Comprehending Spirituals

Understanding Biblical Truth
About the Spiritual Realm

"*It is* the glory of God to conceal a thing:
but the honor of kings *is* to search out a matter."
Proverbs 25:2 (SNT)

James Ross, Ph.D., Thp

To Schedule Dr. Ross, Contact him at:

dimensionalministry@yahoo.com

Table of Contents

Comprehending the Baptism of the Spirit
The Baptism: A Study in the Word
Comprehending the Manifestations of the Spirit
Comprehending Demonic Attacks
Comprehending the word "spirit"
Comprehending the Satanic Attack
Comprehending the Wiles of the Devil
Comprehending Satan's Strategy:
    Phobos -- phobia
    Pagis -- snare
    Noema -- satanic devices, thoughts, and mindsets
    Pathos -- the path temptation
    Oneidismos -- spiritual reproach
Comprehending the Spirit of Anti-Christ
Comprehending the Religious Noema

About the Author

James Ross has been in the Ministry for over thirty years. He received his Ph.D. in 2001 and has taught at the Therapon Institute, Inc., is the President of Dimensional Ministry, holds Pastors Conferences, Revivals, Discipleship Workshops, and has authored several books, which include *Spiritual Foundation*, *Good Grace*, and *The Simplified New Testament*. Dr. Ross and his wife, Sandra, live in Central Texas. They have four children and three grandchildren.

Introduction

During my more than thirty years of ministry I have had many people ask me about "spirituals." The Bible has much to say about them, but it seems the subject is a bit taboo in some circles. I believe this is true because so much of the Church has been duped in believing the "hype" about the subject, they have heard some of the wall doctrines concerning them, or the information they have received was just wrong; biblically speaking. Back in my early years of ministry I became very interested in the subject, but the denomination I was in actually feared the subject. I learned extremely fast that if you even tried to bring the subject up you could lose your pastorate. Once I went to Bible College I discovered that many of the ministerial students would do their best to crucify you as well. I thought that Christians were the ones who sought out truth, and I was right. Once I started Pastoring, even though the subject was a dangerous one, I wanted to do my part to prepare the local church to understand these things. I studied the subject with intensity and before long I began to think that I was an expert on the subject. Boy was I wrong! The more I studied and preached on the subject, the more questions came my way. The statement, "I don't know if I can answer that!" became all too common for me. Over the years I have become a bit more familiar with the topic, even though I will be the first to tell you I believe there is more to the subject than I have discovered. But I do believe if you want to understand the spiritual realm, this is a good book to read. I am a bit biased about it though. My approach is simple. Because I have heard various takes on the matter and have listened to countless people tell me what they think about it; I take an exegetical approach. You see, I want to know the truth. I honestly have to say don't tell me what you think, tell me what the Word of God says about this subject, keep it in context with the Scriptures, and then I will listen. I do not intend to be demeaning. But I have heard some pretty off the wall stuff in my day. I have tried to cover many of the subjects in this work that I feel is necessary to lead people to truth about the subject. I want to do three things in this book. First, I want to cover many of the subjects that I am most often asked about (*the baptism of the Holy Spirit, demonism, and the spirit of the antichrist*). Second, I want to bring the reader to the Word of God for the answers, and third, I want to cover some material that I rarely hear on the subject. This is a good resource for Pastors and church leaders, but is also an excellent text for someone who wants to learn more about the subject.

Comprehending the Baptism of the Spirit

There are many differences of opinion with the issue of how and when Christians receive "the baptism" of the Holy Spirit. Some believe that the Holy Spirit is only received at the time of salvation, while others believe the Holy Spirit is received in a later event. When do we receive the Holy Spirit? What is the evidence of this reception? And how one gets baptized in the Holy Spirit are some of the questions that will be addressed in this chapter. There are also some clarifications that should be made in the beginning of this study for the sake of simplicity. First of all, one cannot be saved unless the Father draws them to Himself by and through the Holy Spirit (see John 6:44, 65). Secondly, the Holy Spirit has not come to glorify Himself; He has come to glorify Jesus (see John 16:14). And third, we receive the Holy Spirit and are sealed by Him at the time of salvation (see Ephesians 1:13).

God is a Spirit and it is his Spirit that inhabits our lives at our new birth in Christ. Salvation cannot occur without the presence of the Holy Spirit, because it is He who quickens our spirit and who gives us spiritual life (see Romans 8:11, Ephesians 2:5 & 1 Peter 3:18). God is not three different Gods, He is one God who has three distinct manifestations of Himself (see Deuteronomy 6:4; Mark 12:29; Galatians 3:20; Ephesians 4:6; James 2:19 and Matthew 28:19). He is God the Father, the Originator of the plan of creation. He is Jesus Christ, the Incarnate God, manifested in the form of man and who is the Creator of all things (see Colossians 1:16-17). And He is the Holy Spirit, God's own person in Spirit form who dwells with us and is in us.

It is not the Holy Spirit's intention to accentuate His coming over the ministry of Jesus. Neither is it the Holy Spirit's intention to accentuate His manifestations over the work of God the Father. The Holy Spirit's role is defined in John 14:26 and John 15:8-11. As He enters the heart of mankind our spirit is quickened (i.e., *made alive*) and His presence in our lives makes us one with Him so that He can do a work in our person. These issues should not be in question. When you are asked, "When do you receive the Holy Spirit?" You should answer, "When I received Jesus." Now the question remains, do we get *all* of the Holy Spirit at one time or are there subsequent and additional fillings that come at a later time? This is the issue that is often misrepresented or that some are confused about. As a Pastor

I once asked a congregation, "Has anyone ever told you to be filled with the Holy Spirit?" They all answered, "Yes!" I then asked, "Has anyone ever told you how to be filled with the Holy Spirit?" They all answered "No!" I read Luke 11:13 and they were amazed that the Bible says you "ask" for Him. I have also ministered to some groups who believe you have to "tarry" and speak in tongues before the Holy Spirit is present. This is also not a biblically accurate description of how we receive the Holy Spirit (see 1 Corinthians 12:29-30 -- *the implied answer is no to each of the questions asked in this passages*). One thing is necessary if you want to receive more of God's presence in your life; you have to want more, but the Scripture also states: "To whom much is given, much is also required."

Believers who have not been trained in spirituals struggle with this subject in many ways. They hear or read about the baptism in the Spirit from many theological perspectives. My purpose is to bring an exegetical study to this subject and to use only the Bible as my source of truth. Others just walk away from a discussion about the matter, while others promote a denominational stance and apply personal preference to their study of the baptism in the Holy Spirit. Paul said on several occasions, "I would not have you to be ignorant" (i.e., *without the knowledge of a subject*). This was his initial and opening statement before he began his instructions to the believers in 1 Corinthians 12. He said this because in his day, just as in ours, too many Christians do not understand spirituals.

The Baptism: A Study in the Word

The New Testament is very clear on the subject of the baptism of the Spirit and spiritual matters as well. The Bible is also clear that the reception of the Holy Spirit occurs more than just at the salvation experience. As we review the Bible on this subject, we should guard our hearts from traditional thinking. Traditional thinking has caused many believers to err from the truth and also causes many to get involved in division, which then gives place to the spirit of anti-Christ. Let's review several passages on this subject.

"Then said Jesus to them again, Peace *be* unto you:
as *my* Father hath sent me, even so send I you. And
when he had said this, he breathed on *them,* and
saith unto them, Receive ye the Holy Ghost."
(John 20:21-22 KJV)

"Jesus said to them again, Peace *be* to you: as *my* Father has sent me,
even so I send you. And when he had said this, he breathed on *them,*
and said to them, You receive the Holy Spirit *right now!*"
(John 20:21-22 SNT)

"And, behold, I send the promise of my Father upon you:
but tarry ye in the city of Jerusalem, until ye be endued
with power from on high."
(Luke 24:49 KJV)

"And, behold, I put in you the promise of my Father (*the Holy
Spirit*): but you wait in the city of Jerusalem, until you are endued
(*clothed*) with *the* power *of the Spirit* from on high."
(Luke 24:49 SNT)

I included the *Simplified King James New Testament* and the *King James Version* to help you to gain clarify on the initial reception of the Holy Spirit. These two passages sum up the first time the disciples received the Holy Spirit; one from the Apostle John's perspective and the other from Luke's perspective. This was on the first day of Jesus' Resurrection, forty-seven days before the Holy Spirit manifested Himself again on the day of Pentecost. The timeline mentioned above is when Jesus came into the upper room with His disciples. Jesus was in the grave the two nights before, then appears in the upper room on Sunday, gives the Holy Spirit to the disciples, and then tells them to wait until Pentecost for the empowering which was to come upon them as well. Luke separated the "promise of the Father" event from the "empowering of the Holy Spirit" that occurred in Acts 2:1-6. Luke is saying that he researched the coming of the Holy Spirit, and he found that an additional distribution of power came upon the disciples during Pentecost that was different from the Upper Room experience. This "clothing of power" is what is commonly termed as the "baptism of the Holy Ghost." We also see this with Apollos and the disciples in Acts 18:24-28 and Acts 19:1-7. Take note of several things in these passages: first, Apollos was fervent in the spirit (see 18:25), but he had only received the baptism of John. Second, Aquila and Priscilla "declared the way of God to him in a more perfect *way*" (see 18:26). And third, when Paul met him he recognized that he had not been "baptized" with the Holy Spirit (see 19:2-6). We will look at the "baptism" of the Holy Spirit later in this chapter.

The King James Bible uses the English word "endued" to express the idea of the "filling" of the Holy Spirit. The Greek word *enduo*, from where "endued" was translated, means "to sink into a garment," or "to endow (*cover*) with clothing." The word carries the idea of putting something on. In Matthew 6:25 and Mark 6:9, *enduo* is translated as "to put on," and in 2 Corinthians 5:3, *enduo* is translated as "being clothed" in the King James Version. This idea of "being clothed" is revealing how we put on our spiritual house that is from heaven; our new man so to speak. The idea of "being clothed" with the "power from on high" simply means "to be invested with heavenly internal power." This is the reality of putting the new man on. This is allowing our Father to enter His house and to set up residence and is why Acts 1:8 (SNT) states:

"But you will receive power, after the Holy Spirit has come on you: and you will be witnesses to me both in Jerusalem, and in all *of* Judea, and in Samaria, and to the farthest part of the earth."

These verses tell us that we will receive this power after the Holy Spirit is present in our life. It is not that you get "all" of the Holy Spirit you are going to get at your salvation experience, nor do you receive "all" of the Holy Spirit in the baptism. Luke states that you have the presence of the Holy Spirit, and then there is an additional "promise of power" that will come at your "feast of Pentecost." But

10

let me add one more thing. In Acts 4:31 (SNT) we see the Apostles and some of the other disciples of Jesus receiving yet another "filling" of the Holy Spirit.

> "And when they had prayed, the place was shaken where they were assembled together; and they were all filled (*influenced*) by the Holy Spirit, and they spoke the word of God with boldness."

Luke testified that the Apostles and other disciples received the Holy Spirit on three different occasions. Luke's understanding of the baptism was that we receive the power from on high as an expression of becoming witnesses to the fact that Christ is alive and lives within us. Luke's proximity to the Churches first Pentecostal experience and his understanding of the baptism is proof enough that "tongues" were not viewed in the first century Church to be the *primary* evidence of the reception. The baptism was not signified, in itself, by the power to speak in tongues (*even though tongues were manifested*); it was a baptism that manifested in the power to be a witness (i.e., *a martyr, or one who bears record of the Lord*). This premise is also stated in Acts 5:32 (SNT),

> "And we are his witnesses concerning these things;
> and the Holy Spirit is also *giving evidence*, which
> God has given to the ones that obey him."

The Greek word *martus* in the first century was a word that is defined as "a legal witness at a trial." A *martus* (*martyr*), as defined, was one who could testify for, collaborate the testimony of the one tried, or who could verify the testimony of another. When Alexander the Great had the Old Testament translated into the Greek language, the word *martus* was used in Isaiah 43:10 and 12, and in 44:8 (SNT) and it was also used as the word "witnesses." Make a note of how Isaiah used the term *witnesses* and what kind of witnesses these were in the passage below.

"Ye are my witnesses (*martus*), saith the Lord, and my servant whom I have chosen; that ye may know and believe me, and understand that I am he: before me there was no God formed, neither shall there be after me…I have declared, and have saved, and I have showed, when there was no strange god among you: therefore ye are my witnesses (*martus*), saith the Lord, that I am God…Fear ye not, neither be

11

afraid: have not I told thee from that time, and have declared it? Ye are my witnesses (*martus*). Is there a God beside me? Yea, there is no God; I know not any." (KJV)

Each of these verses gives evidence that these *witnesses* were to give testimony that God is the "alive" God, and there is no other God but Him. In the time when men believed in gods, gods, and more gods, the pagans needed to understand that there is only one true God. The same holds true today. When every "religion" under the sun is being promoted in our society, it is vitally important that we are the "witnesses" of the One true God. God has made Himself known in Jesus Christ, and we are to declare the fact that we witnessed His manifestation in us. We live by faith in Him and in our understanding about Him. The promise of the Holy Spirit's coming was and is the evidence of Jesus' victory. Acts 2 is a confirmation of Jesus' promise stated in John 14:7 that He was going to send the Comforter. When Jesus said this about the coming Comforter, He was speaking of the Pentecostal event. In John 7:39 it is stated that the Holy Spirit was not yet given because Jesus had not yet been glorified. The act of Jesus returning to the Father was the final step in His glorification and thus the Holy Spirit could then come upon the Church. When the Holy Spirit came in Acts chapter two, He demonstrated all nine manifestations found in 1 Corinthians 12:7-11. Each of the manifestations of the Spirit can be found in the first five chapters of the book of Acts. Even though tongues manifested first, it does not signify that it is *the* evidence of the baptism. In fact, the first miracle was that the disciples were in one accord! Luke's purpose was not to glorify tongues. His purpose was to bear witness that the Holy Spirit was establishing the Kingdom of God (see Acts 1:2-3). The chart below is but a brief look at how Luke bore witness to all nine of these manifestations in the book of Acts. Compare the list to 1 Corinthians 12:7-10.

Acts 2:3—tongues
Acts 2:8-11—interpretation of tongues
Acts 3:6-9—healing
Acts 3:10—faith
Acts 3:17—word of knowledge
Acts 4:8-10—word of wisdom
Acts 4:22—miracles (also in Acts 5:12)
Acts 4:24-30—prophecy
Acts 5:1-4—discernment

Luke also testifies that during the forty days that Jesus remained on the earth after His resurrection, He gave commandments to the first Apostles. One of these commandments (see Acts 1:4-5) was for them to wait in Jerusalem for "the promise of the Father," which was then identified as the baptism of the Holy Spirit. They had already received the Holy Spirit (see John 20:22 and Luke 24:49), but they had not yet been "enabled with the power from on high." And they received another "filling" in Acts 4:31. For the sake of definition and clarity to be a witness is "the ability to tell people about Jesus," which is your testimony, but a witness is also someone who has experienced salvation and the presence of the living God, and who can confirm that He is God with their life, as well as with their tongue. It is with our tongue that we bear witness that He is our Lord. Our "tongue" reveals who rules your life. It is with the tongue that everyone around me will know whether I am godly or whether I have a filthy mouth. It is with the tongue that many bless and with the same tongue they curse. You can speak about God and/or speak in tongues, and still not know Him in His fullness, but one cannot be a witness without the experience of His Presence.

There are several times in the book of Acts where different people received the baptism of the Holy Spirit. Each of these receptions is unique. There may be some commonality in these events, but that is not to be construed as a systematic formula in the baptism of the Holy Spirit. One is filled with the Holy Spirit when they have the faith and desire to receive Him, they ask for His presence in their life, and then God will "fill" anyone when they desire more of His Presence. For example:

John 20:22 and Luke 24:49: The Apostles and other disciples received the Holy Spirit
Acts 2:1-6: The Apostles and other disciples received the baptism of the Spirit; no hands were laid on them; *evidence that they received*: tongues and interpretation
Acts 4:31: The third reception of the Apostles and other disciples; no hands were laid on them; *evidence that they received*: boldness
Acts 8:17: The Samaritans were filled; hands were laid on them; *evidence*: none given
Acts 9:17: Paul was filled; hands laid on him; *evidence that he received*: scales fell off his eyes

13

Acts 10:44: Cornelius and first Gentiles filled; no hands were laid on them; *evidence that they received*: tongues and faith

Acts 13:52: Gentiles filled again; no hands mentioned; *evidence that they received*: joy

Acts 19:6: Apollos and his company filled; hands were laid on them; *evidence that they received*: tongues and prophecy

The real issue here is we can be filled with God's Spirit and the manifestations of His presence are available to us. It is a matter of choice and capacity. You will never operate in the manifestations of the Spirit if you do not choose to. How much of the Holy Spirit are you capable of walking in? Look at it this way: A pint jar can be filled and it will be full, but a quart has more capacity than a pint. Pour the "fullness" of the pint into the quart and it does not "fill" it up completely. Simply stated, the quart has more capacity than the pint and so it is with Christians. Some people have less capacity than others; it is a matter of faith. Each of us have a certain capacity and God will fill you to your capacity; if you so desire to be filled. But our capacity can be enlarged and should be as we increase our faith. Some Christians have little faith, in other words, they have little capacity, while others have a greater capacity or faith. Greater faith, greater capacity. Jesus commanded us to go from "faith to faith" (see Romans 1:17) and also from "glory to glory" (see 2 Corinthians 3:18). Less capacity means you do not desire to go to a greater level of glory in God. It all depends on how much you are willing to lay down your life, and take on the life of Christ. Many in the First Century Church received three "fillings" (*thirty, sixty, and a hundred-fold*), because "they did not love their lives (*souls or inner self will*) even to the death." (see Revelation 12:11).

The baptism of the Holy Spirit is clearly defined in the New Testament as occurring after the disciples and others received an initial filling, so to speak. The issue is then, how much have you opened up your heart to the Lord? Again, what is your spiritual capacity? You can either be a pint, a quart, or a gallon. You may be full as a quart, but the gallon has a greater capacity than the quart and is available as you open your heart to God. It is all about allowing God to expand your heart. To whom much is given, much is also required. If you want to be expanded in spiritual matters, you must open your heart to what God has for you. The truth is if you do not open the door when Jesus is knocking, you will not receive anything from Him.

14

Comprehending the Manifestations of the Spirit

When trying to understand the manifestations of the Holy Spirit, a simple reviewing of the Scriptures is the best approach. The Church is rich in manifestations and gifts, but there are many things that are scandalously out of order in it. A sound doctrinal framework is necessary if we are to understand the function and purpose the list of spirituals found in 1 Corinthians 12:8-10 contain. First of all, these expressions of the spirit are not "gifts," they are called the "manifestations" by Paul and there is a difference between manifestations and gifts (compare 1 Corinthians 12:7 and Romans 12:6-8). These are called "manifestations," but to better understand the nature of the manifestations, they are defined as the "exhibitions" or "expressions" of the Spirit's inner "working on our mind." The Greek word *phanerosis* (*translated as manifestations*) actually tells us that the purpose of these spiritual manifestations are to "make it apparent that the Spirit of God is in us." Barnes describes this phenomenon this way:

"The idea here is, that there is given to those endowments, or graces as shall "manifest" the work and nature of the Spirit's operations on the mind; such endowments as the Spirit makes himself known through people. All that he produces in the mind is a manifestation of his character and work, in the same way as the works of God in the visible creation are a manifestation of his perfections."

This Greek word *phanerosis* (*manifestation*) is only used twice in the New Testament. In 2 Corinthians 4:2 (SNT) it is used in the context of "rendering apparent" the truth.

"But have renounced the hidden things of dishonesty, not walking in craftiness (*subtlety*), or handling the word of God deceitfully; but by the manifestation (*expression*) of the truth commending (*introducing*) ourselves to every man's conscience in the sight of God."

The manifestations of the Spirit are a part of the Christian experience for personal profit or benefit (see 1 Corinthians 12:7). Satan has used our lack of understanding, (*where the manifestations are concerned*), to hinder the clarity of God's Word and to produce division. The Greek word translated as "profit" is *sumphero* (1 Corinthians 12:7). This word means "to bear together; i.e., to bring together, and to collect or contribute in order to help." These manifestations profit or help us in what way? They help us to contribute to the union and maturity within the Body of Christ. Christ came to save us and to make us one. This is why Paul declares that we are One Body in 1 Corinthians 12:12-30. Isn't it amazing that Satan uses them to create division when their purpose is unity! The manifestations are given to bring us together, not to divide us. Satan always comes to steal, kill, and destroy the work of God. This is why pride has continued to separate the Body of Christ into sectarianistic denominations. Pride is the *phanerosis* of Satan, and separation is the evidence of its work. Now to the question, how many manifestations can I have? 1 Corinthians 12:11 states,

> "But everyone of these are activated by the Spirit himself,
> distributing to everyone personally as he desires."
> (SNT)

How are they divided (i.e., *distributed*)? They are divided or received as the person *wills*. Some believe the manifestations are divided as the Holy Spirit *wills*. The Holy Spirit is the worker of these manifestations. These are the manifestations of Who He Is, but it is the person's *will* that releases or hinders the functioning of these manifestations. If you want to speak in tongues you will; if you refuse to speak in tongues, you will not. It is up to you. The Lord intended for these manifestations to be utilized. They are available for our profit and benefit, yet one group will emphasize tongues, the next will emphasize faith, and still the next will emphasize prophecy. Each group has their favorite manifestation, and each group has the same problem, they all exalt one manifestation over the other. These manifestations have the same purpose. They are to profit the individual and to bring the group into unity. By example, some exalt one "operations" gift over another (see Ephesians 4:8 and 11). These gifts (*the English word "gift" is translated from the Greek word "doma"*) are the Apostles, the Prophets, the Evangelists, and the Teaching Pastor. The Greek word *doma* is also defined as "a covering;" like an umbrella (i.e., *a dome*). Each *doma* office has its purpose and place. A Christian cannot be completely equipped unless they experience the anointing of each of the *doma* functions, because they each minister to a specific area of our spirit (see Ephesians 4:12). These *doma* gifts function specifically in the Body of Christ for very practical reasons. Apostolic and prophetic ministries are foundational anointings (see Ephesians 2:20), while the evangelist and the teaching shepherd have "maintenance ministries." Apostolic and prophetic ministries build stability into our life, while the evangelists and the teaching shepherds maintain the integrity and function that was established by the foundational ministries. Evangelists are designed by God to teach the babes in the faith. Apostles and prophets teach foundational doctrines and deal with carnality and maturity issues. Teaching Pastors are like shepherds of old; they live with and lead God's people throughout their journey of faith. Teaching Pastors are also guides and counselors, giving advice and feeding the flocks, while Apostles and Prophets are fathers who train our souls, correcting us, and set the spiritual course as the Holy Spirit leads. Evangelists aid in the birthing and growth of the babes in Christ, passing them "under the hand" to the other *doma* or covering gifts God has established in the Church. We will take a more in depth look at each of these ministries in a later chapter.

Each of the manifestations has purpose. For example, tongues are for those who lack faith in their life. Tongues are faith builders. This is why Jude 20 (SNT) states,

> "But you, beloved, build up yourselves in your
> consecrated faith, praying in the Holy Spirit
> (*Praying "restfully" within the Holy Spirit.*)."

This is why tongues are a sign to those of less faith (*"...who believe not"*) and not to the faithful (see 1 Corinthians 14:22). Jude gives us a bit of clarity about tongues when he says "praying in the Holy Ghost." Paul, in the instruction he gave in 1 Corinthians 14:15 (SNT) uses the term "praying with" the Holy Spirit and declares,

> "What is it then? I will pray with the spirit, and I will pray with the understanding (*mind or thoughts*) also: I will sing with the spirit, and I will sing with the understanding (*mind or thoughts*) also."

Praying "with" or "in" the Holy Spirit is a key to understanding this manifestation. The Corinthians did not comprehend the manifestations of the Spirit or their purposes. We are much the same. There is a difference between praying "with" or praying "in" the Spirit, and being "in the Spirit" when we pray. We should all make sure we are "in" the Spirit when we pray, whether we are praying in tongues or with our understanding. We should take heed to the admonition to the Church to change our ways and change our attitudes about these wonderful manifestations the Spirit of God has

17

graced us with. We should no longer exalt one manifestation over the other just as we should not forbid them. If we can make this transition, the Kingdom of God will draw one step closer to becoming a living reality in our lives. Paul's counsel is simple:

> "Therefore, brothers, desire to prophesy, and do not forbid *people* to speak in languages. Let everything be accomplished decently and in order."
> (1 Corinthians 14:39-40 SNT)

You may not speak in tongues, but it is still the admonition of the Bible that teaches us to not "forbid" their manifestation. When we thoroughly study the manifestations we will find that they are for "private" use, while the spiritual gifts found in Romans 12 are for public use. Public use of the manifestations is one of the reasons there has been controversy about this subject. This is most likely the major point of clarity in understanding the manifestations and the spiritual gifts. This is why Paul clearly states that he prefers to use a "known" language in the public arena.

Why are so many people ignorant of spirituals? Mostly because groups have promoted false concepts about the manifestations, which in turn has produced fear in other Christians who do not understand their purpose or who have not experienced their proper operation. One group promotes their *belief*, while yet another group promotes their personal preference about the manifestations. They war over who is right, but the end result is disunity in the Church and misunderstanding of the manifestations and their function in the Body of Christ. God's people should be trained in spirituals and read their Bibles. That way we will all understand the reality and function of the manifestations and their purpose in us individually.

Comprehending Demonic Attacks

The primary thing about most teaching on demonism and demonology is that they both generally look at demonic activity in a specific way. The Church has been trained over many years to view demonology in the "Exorcist" way, if I may. The thing to know about Satan and his dominions is that they work on us *indirectly* 99.99% of the time.

Not every situation or problem in life has a demonic root, but Satan and his demonic forces are a reality in this life The first place to start in understanding demonic attacks is to know what a demonic *spirit* is. Many view these beings in light of pagan philosophy, rather than from an exegetical and biblical standpoint. Early European pagan religions and some forms of Greek philosophy breed the ideas of ghosts and goblins, which is not in line with Scriptural truth. Jesus and the Apostles viewed demons as "beings that had knowledge" or "were experienced in a thing." This is why the Greek word *diamon* (*demon*) was used to describe them. The root meaning of the Greek word translated as *demon* comes from a word that means "to assign," hence the concept of satanic assignment or appointment is derived. From the outset of this study we must recognize a simple truth concerning demons. There are only two ways an individual can experience demonic oppression on a constant basis. The first is a lack of Christian maturity, and the other is to not know Christ Jesus as Savior. This is not to say that if you experience demonic attacks you are immature. I am simply stating that when an individual cannot defeat demonic advancements it is due to spiritual immaturity.

"And the seventy returned again with joy, saying, Lord, even the devils are subject to us through your name. And he said to them, I watched Satan fall from heaven like lightning. Behold, I give to you *the* ability to tread on serpents and scorpions (*devils and demons*), and over all the power of the enemy: and nothing at all will hurt you. Rather do not rejoice in this, that the spirits are subordinate to you; but rather rejoice, because your names are written in heaven. In that instant Jesus rejoiced in spirit, and said, I thank you, O Father, Lord of heaven and earth, that you have hidden these things from the wise and prudent and have revealed them to babies: even so, Father; because it seemed so good in your sight."
(Luke 10:17-21 SNT)

He that is in you is greater than he that is in the world (see 1 John 4:4). Notice that Jesus identified the disciples as "babes" when he prayed for them, because even the weakest Christian is stronger than the strongest devil.

Comprehending the word "spirit"

The word "spirit" in the New Testament (*pneuma*) is defined in the Strong's Concordance as "a current of air (i.e. *breath, a blast, or a breeze*)." The word can be literally defined from Greek exegesis as "to give life to" something. We should be aware that the word *pneuma*, as defined in the context of the human soul, is described as "the vital principle of life," or "a mental disposition," and *pneuma* has been interpreted as the *spirit* of a man, or as the Spirit of God, and paradoxically as a demon or an angel (*also a spiritual being*)." There are only two Greek words, in the New Testament, that are translated as the English word "spirit(s)"; they are *pneuma* and the word *phantasma*. *Phantasma* is only used twice in the New Testament, in Matthew 14:26 and Mark 6:49. The word describes the idea of a "being that is spiritual by nature," whether a demon or a being of another sort. The writers of the New Testament used the word *phantasma* to describe their attitudes when they saw Jesus walking on the water; they thought He was a "spirit." I will define and explain *pneuma* throughout this chapter.

To better understand the influence of demonic beings in our lives we must first know how they affect us. There are two ways that Satan attacks people: by "direct" demonic oppression and through "indirect" demonic oppression. The Scripture prepares us to combat these attacks and gives us the wisdom to see their encroachment. We need to be aware of several phases involved in Satan's approach. These phases are described by the Greek words: *topos, methodia, pagis, noema, phobos, pathos,* and *oneidismos*. When these Greek words are translated they reveal how Satan takes an overview (*topos*) of our life. He then devises a method (*methodia*) of attack by using a snare (*pagis*) that is triggered by a demonic device (*noema*) that produces fear (*phobos*) in an area of our soul, which then results in a pattern of thought or *phobia*, which in turn, creates a path (*pathos*) or way of life (*lifestyle*) that results in reproach (*oneidismos*).

Comprehending the Satanic Attack

"Neither give opportunity or occasion to the devil.."
(Ephesians 4:27 SNT)

The Greek word *topos*, translated as "place" in the King James version and is translated by the words "opportunity" and "occasion" in the above passage, and means "to give a condition to, to create an opportunity for, or to give a license" to the devil that makes an attack possible. The Bible teaches us to not give Satan an opportunity or an occasion that he can use to his advantage. *Topos* is where the English word "top" originates. To be on top is to have the "advantage by position." Webster's dictionary defines the word *top* as "the highest part of anything; the highest rank," or it is also described as "a platform with the most prominent view." Militarily speaking, whosoever holds the high ground has the advantage. Satan's plan is to gain a position over us that gives him the most strategic perspective of our life. *Topographein* is another Greek word that means "to describe a place" and is a derivative of *topos*. This is where the word "topography" originates. To take a topographical survey is the art or practice of graphing the "delineation of a land's natural features." It is most commonly understood to be a picture of the ground taken from above. This picture from above shows the layout of that property with its boundaries, as well as its natural features. Satan wants to gain the advantage in order to view us in this way. He surveys us from birth to discover our natural vulnerabilities and weaknesses (*Satan uses "familiar" or family spirits to accomplish this goal*). These delineations or diagrams of our tendencies can then be utilized for our demise. Think about the way you are in a natural sense. Do you anger quickly? Your children will too. Are you fearful? You will see the transference of these natural tendencies into your family. We are commanded in the Scriptures to be aware of our natural tendencies that give Satan and his forces place or opportunity (i.e., *topos*). We should not give him a license or set up the right condition for him to attack us. For example, if we open the door to lust, Satan sees the opportunity and can take advantage of us with this knowledge. If we have natural tendencies, that is, if we have a common disposition or an inclination toward something, Satan will send someone or something to fulfill that desire in us. Eve gave Satan the opportunity to deceive her when she gave him "place". How did it happen? She gave him place simply by listening to him. When Eve listened she gave Satan access into her thoughts and her reasoning. We can remove this *topos* from Satan through the authority of Jesus Christ and by being obedient to the Word of God. Satan does not have the right to trespass because the work of the cross removed his power over us. We have been redeemed by the Lord and purchased by His blood, so Satan has no right to manipulate us. But remember, Satan is a thief and a robber, and robbers break the law. See Deuteronomy 18:10-13 for a limited list of demonic spirits and manifestations.

Satan and his fallen angels have been cast down. When Satan wants to violate you and create vulnerability in you, he sends a demonic spirit to affect a certain thing that he sees in you. When you realize that a demonic spirit is a being that "gives life" to something in you, it will renew your mind and give you revelation, and you will be able to connect the dots, so to speak. For example, it is the Spirit of God who gives life to our spirit and when our spirit is "quickened" (i.e., *made alive*); it becomes the source of strength for the inner, hidden man of the heart. We then have access to God because we have given place to Jesus Christ, who is the door (see John 10:9 and Revelation 3:8). When a demonic spirit comes from Satan, it gives life to something that produces the fruit of the flesh or promotes the wisdom that is from below (see James 3:15). Satan establishes a doorway through the soul to worldliness. The doorway or *principality* is part of Satan's method (see Ephesians 6:11-12). This earthliness (*worldliness*) is Satan's ability to create a connection between your soul (*your mind, your will, and/or your temperament*) and a worldly life viewpoint. Through this doorway Satan then builds a stronger demonic merger by combining sensuality and worldliness, thus reinforcing his position of control. This sensuality is called *psuchikos* in the Greek language. When *psuchikos* (i.e., *selfishness or self-amplification*) is utilized, it produces a selfishly motivated and self-centered person that Satan can then fabricate into a "devilish individual" (*diamonizomai*). A point of interest for every Christian to consider is when *diamonizomai* is discovered in someone, we should realize that their personal foundation is not complete.

Diamonizomai is the Greek word that means "to be demonized." It is the oppression that occurs in the life of an individual who has been under attack for long periods of time. Oppression is defined as "the depression of mind or spirit." The Greek word gives us a picture of one who is "vexed" or is "under the power of a demon." *Diamonizomai* (i.e., *oppression*) can cause afflictions in the body

23

and/or the mind according to the Scriptures. The Scripture attributes paralysis, blindness, and deafness as well as loss of speech, epilepsy, melancholy, and insanity to *diamonizomai*. The concept of possession should not be associated with this. Demons do not possess; that is pagan ideology, not original Christian theology. They control by manipulation and deception. Demons cannot possess the freewill of a person. That would give us an excuse for our actions and "the devil made me do it" ideology would then be a reality. This is not so. Demons control by taking the advantage *topos* gives them, but Satan's scheme is to make you think that his thought, which he has implanted in your mind, are your thoughts or are how you really are. If you are deceived into giving Satan greater control, you can, if you choose to, but Satan's scheme is to make you think that his thoughts, which he has implanted in your mind, are your thoughts or are how you really are. Demons express themselves in the consciousness of a person by two means: direct and indirect manifestation. Direct demonic influence (*manifestation*) occurs when spirits are openly manifesting their influence in a person by manipulating the individual's temperament, and by perverting a person's disposition and thought processes. The level of this manifestation is directly proportional to the amount of "place" a person gives the demonic spirit. The degree of *topos* given to demons by an individual can reflect in the intensity of the manipulation it uses. It can reach the level of oppression the Gadarene demonic walked in, as seen in Mark 5. This oppression manifested and caused him to hurt himself, becoming antisocial, as well as being obsessed with death and dying. Matthew 4:24 reveals that when someone is "demonized" it can make them sick. The Greek words translated as "sick" people in this passage describes people who are held in a condition of oppression. Direct contact with demon spirits creates an inner pathway whereby they have opened the way for this type of manipulation. Again, we all have free will and no demon can control the will, but an individual can give such place to a devil that the devil freely utilizes the person's faculties, and this is evidenced in the Scriptures. We see many examples of this in our society. Mass murderers, parents killing their children, children killing other children and so on. When people give place to the devil, they open their minds to various perverted thought processes, as well as unrealistic "truths." I knew a man once whose wife called me and asked if I would come and get her because her husband thought she had a devil when she would not do something he asked her to. He opened his mind to evil thoughts and tried to literally "beat the devil out of her;" no pun intended.

In Mark 5 the Gadarene demoniac had several characteristics that should be noted. These characteristics are common among individuals who have direct demonic influence in their lives. First, he had an unnatural association with death (*he was a man of the tombs*). The Greek word translated as "tombs" has the root meaning of "remembering" or "to remember something that was traumatic." The word "tomb" is defined as a *cenotaph* (i.e., *a monument for someone not buried at that place*). We see them all the time as we travel down major highways or other roads. Little crosses on the side of the road signifying that someone has died there in a car accident is a *cenotaph*. The Gadarene was obsessed with death and dying, and is described as having such demonic influence in his life that he hurt himself. Self-mutilation is a common characteristic of demonically manipulated people. Most often it is a cry for attention, but when someone cuts himself it is also evidence of a much deeper and sinister situation. The Gadarene was also out of control. He was defiant and could not be restrained. Satanic influence manifests in people as unruliness, defiance, rebelliousness, hatred for authority figures, and disobedience. People who are under direct demonic influence most often reflect and manifest Satan's personality. They are pride filled and arrogant, hostile to authority, abusive, cruel, and violent.

In Mark 5 the devils described themselves by the Greek word *polus* (i.e., *many*). The common interpretation of "legion" is that it represents a certain number of devils, but the word means much more than a number. It means "great or strong," and carries the idea of something that is prolific. The passage could have easily been translated with the phrase, "we are legion, for we rule this man like an army occupies the land." The level of demonic control also relates directly to salvation. When salvation is present the level of control is generally less than when one is not saved. The demons begged the Lord not to send them out of the *chora* (*country*). The root meaning of this word is "an empty place" or "a chasm," which is one of the hidden descriptions of hell. These devils had found some unoccupied territory in the man's life that was easily exploited. Every lost person has a "void" in their heart. When it is not filled by the Holy Spirit, Satan takes up residence. Though demonic influence is a biblical reality, demonic rule should not be found in the lives of those who know God as Savior. I say "should not," because Christians can give place to the devil. James, John, and Peter all did (see Matthew 16:23 and Luke 9:53-54). The Gadarene had given place to a large number, of what the New Testament describes, as "unclean spirits." *Topos* was given to the devils in such a degree that they ruled him (see Mark 5:8). In other words, the man's thoughts were totally out of the normal range, which then led him to activities that manifested his fears, at least in his own mind.

When demonic spirits come to us, they come with a purpose. An "unclean" spirit comes to "give life to" impurity or lewdness within the individual. Child molesters and other such behavior has its roots in this type of demonic mindset. The unclean spirit is associated with idolatry throughout the Bible. The Old Testament, in its practical approach to the salvation, deals with demonic influence from their origin. Of course Satan is ultimately the originator, but he uses anything he can as a "producer." Rejection gives place to unclean spirits and unclean spirits thrive on the emotions that are related to insecurity.

One common cause of rejection is incest. When a person has experienced incest, self-rejection manifests through shame and an imposed impure disposition, which directly relates to the self worth. When we look at Tamar (see 2 Samuel 13) we can see the progression of this problem in her personality. Incest produces shame, then rejection, and finally a bi-polar state of insanity (see 2 Samuel 13: 16, 19, 20). Demonic forces promote promiscuity and pornography to increase incest. Fornication (*porneia*) gives place to incest, homosexual tendencies, sexual experimentation, and sexual perversion. We also find that a person who is under direct demonic influence is also without restraint (i.e., *control factors*) that govern moral behavior. Their moral point of view has an attitude of lust where anything and everything is acceptable to them. We see this manifesting in our society as we are told that we cannot "judge" others.

Extreme rebelliousness is often the evidence of demonic manipulation. Submission to authority is not in the devil's nature. Every restraint will be tried and tested by demonized individuals. They will use every logical concept and thought to justify their immoral positions and beliefs, and they usually view all outside authority as oppressive. They fight and fear any and every moral control.

The person who is under direct demonic influence will also have tendencies to scream, raise their voice inappropriately, shriek, and throw tantrums. Remember, these individuals are also involved in self-mutilation. I know of a four-year old child who was not allowed to get his way so he cut his own arm to get back at the parent. It is highly unlikely a four-year old would do this type of behavior without some form of outside influence. After the event the child confessed that he cut himself because he "wanted his mommy to give him the candy." This is not to say that out of control children are demonized, but there should be a cause for alarm when extreme behavior has moved into severe and outlandish behavior.

The demonized are often involved in self-destructive behavior. Another manifestation of direct demonic influence is a perverted attitude toward Jesus Christ. Demonically influenced people view God as one who torments them and Christians as people who want to torment them. Their concept of faith is distorted and they tend to get involved in doctrinal extremes.

Indirect demonic influence, on the other hand, is often hidden in the subtleties of one's own personality. Indirect influence is most commonly seen in people who believe a lie and refuse to believe that the lie is a lie. No matter what evidence is presented to them they have a belief or idea that they refuse to see as wrong or distorted. Indirect influence is usually something from one's past which taps into a path of a previous root of pain or trauma, allowing the influence to remain hidden until re-ignited by a present experience. This "path of the root" is our ability to feel an emotion of the past as though it originated in the present. This is how a demonic spirit can affect our present disposition and suddenly bring on a state of depression, anxiety, or a panic attack that seems to occur from out of nowhere in particular. We will more fully develop "the Path of the Root" in a later chapter in this book. These demonic spirits give life to something by tapping into the path that the old root has taken. For example, if you had a bad relationship in the past and meet someone new, Satan can tap into the root and cause you bring up those old feelings when the new person touches that emotional path. It's like someone who went through a bad marriage and their emotions flare up at their new mate even without a cause, or in an extreme case they accuse their new mate of "being just like" their old one. The new spouse may be unaware of the trigger (i.e., *some simple action*) that causes a path of the root when their new husband or wife touches it. I was counseling a couple where the wife had been abused by her former husband and lived in fear of abuse by her new husband. Her new husband was unaware of her fears and would say things that would trigger her emotional state and release unwarranted fear and anger. The problem in their marriage would manifest with little or no reason. The husband would disagree with something the wife said, and she would react very inappropriately and in extremes. Once the path of the root was identified, it could finally be resolved. We should recognize that a spirit of fear breathes or gives life to fear in you or taps the path of an old fear to its source. Each time certain incidents would occur, her emotion would tap into the root of her fear and it would regenerate all the pain she had bottled up inside. Through counseling and love she was able to overcome her past and accept her husband for whom he is, not what she feared him to be. If you listen to the devil and give place to fear then the fear begins to grow. The longer you give place to it, the longer it has the time to sprout roots or return to its old path. When it has not been dealt with properly, it will manifest in multiple and in various ways.

When you do not give Satan entrance, Satan then deceives and manipulates the individual to obtain the best condition for that entrance. Satan is constantly trying to gain access to our heart and mind. If Satan has the "topography" of your life he is able to send these demonic forces to survey and/or attack the weak area he discovers.

Let us review the various demonic influences contained in the Bible. I will only list those and describe the characteristics of the ones that are found in the exegesis of the Scriptures.

By definition a spirit of fear is "a disposition of timidity, faithlessness, dread, fearfulness, or cowardice." By example, a disciple I was training was given instructions to read nine chapters a day in the New Testament. He made excuses for two months how he was unable to follow the instruction. I read the book of Malachi to him in about ten minutes. I was reading very slow and methodically. I showed him that reading at a slow pace took only forty minutes to read nine chapters, give or take a few minutes. He had lost confidence in his ability to read and had created a disposition of inability in himself. He had lived with a degraded view of himself for years and this path had to be broken. He believed the task was too great and he was overwhelmed with the homework. The spirit of fear was defeated by the truth (*A spirit of fear is also defined as "to wax feeble" or "to be weak" due to pride and arrogance.*).

A spirit of perversion is a spirit that introduces a distorted or twisted perspective to an individual. In the Bible this demonic influence is described as "to be a crook, to do amiss, to commit error, to do wrong, and to feel alone." One of the purposes of a spirit of perversion is to cause you to be weighted down with feelings of guilt. This is perversion because Jesus took our sin on Himself. The Bible says that God has cast our sin as far as the east is from the west. Isaiah 19:14 says that a perverted spirit is "mingled" and that this mingling affects every work of God in our lives. A spirit of perversion affects our activities and the operation of our inner self. A manifestation of insecurity is one of the things that will become mingled in our activities if a spirit of perversion is working on us. These levels of insecurity also have an effect on our worldview. When a spirit of perversion and a spirit of fear work in tandem they greatly increase their individual effect. They work to affect the "origin" of our soul's reference point. Demons influence our worldview so that it no longer originates from God centeredness, but stems from self-centeredness. This is one of the things that cause us to do wrong things or commit error. Our thought processes, our will, and our emotions become distorted due to the perversion of perceived self-ability or inability. Satan is then able to introduce error, because from his vantage point he is able to see the shift in our paradigm (*patterns*). An unclean spirit works in close proximity to a perverted spirit and strengthens one's self-centeredness into idolatry. Once Satan has introduced the perversion, he can then mingle demonic, impure, and lewd concepts into the life and thought processes because of his *topos*. When the uncleanness of the demonic spirit begins to take root, self-righteousness is used to shore-up the demonic objectives. The believer becomes uncorrectable because they justify themselves or view others as the problem. They are no longer flexible and adaptable in their responses to the Holy Spirit and thus become rigid and hard-hearted. Satan can now use other demonic forces to complete his invasion and the occupation of their land. When Satan has the *topos* he can view an individual's weaknesses and plan his attacks accordingly. Consider the Pharisees and Sadducees in Jesus' day. Satan had blinded them by pride and self-worth. Satan used their place and stature to the degree that they murdered Jesus.

Familiar spirits are a unique class of demonic forces. There are fifteen different familiar spirits listed in the Bible. They operate in stealth by hiding in custom and tradition. The word "familiar" in the original language means "to talk or chatter in a meaningless or simple-minded way." It is to babble on without purpose. The etymology of the word comes from the Hebrew word that is translated as "father" or "patriarchal." To have a familiar spirit is to have an area in your life that is incomplete (*usually due to improper or ungodly training*), especially when the father in the household does not take an active role in the child's upbringing or does not live up to his responsibility as a dad. When fathers are critical or ignore their children, this in itself increases insecurity and produces a weakened countenance in the child. A *familiar* spirit is a family characteristic that is passed down through the generations, creating a commonality or family distinction. The Bible lists these characteristics as necromancy, an observer of times, an enchanter, a witch, and a wizard. These are very serious and hidden demonic tendencies that originate, at times, in family tradition. I am only dealing with the traditions which are sometimes called "family curses." The characteristic within an individual that causes them to be preoccupied with death and dying is the "necromancing" spirit. This demonic force works commonly with the spirit of fear and influences morbid behavior such as hypochondria and it produces a pathological fear of ill health or unexpected death that will porter (*open the door*) an entrance to sickness. The degree of entrance a necromancing spirit has will dictate the degree of manifestation or affixation in the life of the person. This spirit, when accompanied by a spirit of perversion, also guides individuals into sexual distortions of the grossest kind. Also, let it be understood that necromancing spirits have the ability to produce physical symptoms according to the Bible.

An "observer of times" is a familiar spirit and is one who ritualistically (*almost psychotic at times*) acts covertly. This spirit is a major source of paranoia. The Hebrew word is also translated as "sorcerer" and carries the concept of "one who covers in a demonic way." This covering is the state of mind one gets through horoscopes or through the practicing of spiritualism. It also means "to gather or collect" by using soothsaying. The sorcerer is one who looks for "place" with you so they can control you. In essence they want to be your friend because you have something they want. Once they get it they are usually "finished with your friendship." Individuals with the manifestation of this demonic influence manipulate friendships, coerce opportunities, and use every tactic possible to gain the advantage in relationships. When an individual is unaware of this demonic influence in their life, they tend to feel hostility within personal relationships. These people are usually control freaks. They most often are unaware that their tactics can be seen and the possessiveness they express is repulsive to the non-influenced victim. This demonic spirit has influenced many of America's youth; boyfriend or girl friend control (*which grows stronger in marriage*) is one of the obvious manifestations.

An "enchanter" is one who learns by the experience of omens. An "omen" is a sign or indication of some future event or is an occurrence or phenomenon believed to portend a future event. This is common in many false prophets today. They use their knowledge of an individual or upcoming event to prophesy a course and direction that is not given by God, but through their "senses." These types of prophecies are usually general in nature and open to interpretation. In Genesis 44:5 and 15, Joseph used his cup as a "tool of divining" to get information about his father and brother. Joseph used his cup as a tool to control his brothers' actions in order to get a designed outcome. Joseph's purpose was for the restoration and deliverance of his family, but enchanters do this for profit. The profit an enchanter is looking for does not have to be money. It can be power, position, honor, glory, or recognition. The idea of a "nosy person" is also expressed here. They want information about you so they can use it to their advantage. They will tell another person what they know about you in order to gain stature with them. They also put others down in order to make themselves look better.

The "wizard" and the "witch" are basically the male and the female manifestations of the same familiar spirit, with a few idiosyncrasies particular to each one. The witch, as exegetically described, works to cut off and destroy people by evil speaking. Gossip and backbiting are the two most common manifestations of this demonic influence. Witches have the characteristics that work toward the elimination of a person's authority and effectiveness. They speak curses onto people by announcing their faults and/or failures publicly, as well as privately. Curses do not have to be incantations or spells; they are

31

more commonly misrepresentations of the truth about an individual's character. These words curse individuals by creating a biased image of their character and personage. The Hebrew word for "curses" means "to cut down" or "to cause one to be dismissed." The witch uses these demonic forces to assist her in the exclusion, destabilizing, and removal of authorities and dignities, especially in church life. Lies and falsities produce a hardship of service for church leaders, which in turn, discourages the person from serving God, but that is the purpose of the curse: to destroy their effectiveness. The wizard operates as does the witch, but goes further in his attacks. His level of deception and manipulation is much more severe than the witch. The wizard uses his insight of a person or situation to affect and control it. The Bible teaches us that wizards are lawless and full of iniquities. They use relationships, family problems, dispositions, and attitudes to manipulate their preferred outcome into every situation. Their ability to affect someone is also increased by their position. Familiar spirits use their influence to control an individual in order that their control of one individual will affect others. Notice that these are *familiar* spirits, which means they are most commonly associated with indirect demonic influence, and are commonly propagated in the home or in familiar circumstances.

Comprehending the Wiles of the Devil

> "Put on the whole armor of God, in order that you will be able to stand against the wiles (*methods*) of the devil. Because we do not wrestle against flesh and blood, but against principalities (*demonic magistrates*), against *demonic* authorities, against the *demonic* lords of the darkness of this age, *and* against spiritual malice in heavenly *places*.."
> (Ephesians 6:11-12 SNT)

One of the major errors in Christian circles is that Satan's abilities under-estimated. The degree of cleverness Satan can muster to disguise his real purpose is often extreme and insightful. Our enemy will go to great lengths to out-maneuver us in his attacks. One thing of interest is Paul's choice of words in describing the controlling process. The Greek word translated as "wiles" in Ephesians 6:11 is the word *methodia*. It is where the English word "method" originates. The word means "to travel over, that is, to go systematically to work, to do or pursue something methodically, and according to a set standard of procedure." Satan orderly and meticulously follows a technical procedure in the way he handles of every individual. The same Greek word is also used in Ephesians 4:14 and is translated as to "lie in wait to deceive." This is how Satan attacks. He gets into position and waits on us to show him an area of our lives that is vulnerable. What is he lying in wait for? Remember he is working on us to get the *topos*. He is waiting on an opportunity or a condition to open a way for him to give him an entrance. He is waiting for the demon principalities, the demonic authorities, the demonic rulers of the darkness of this world, and the wicked spirits in the heavenly places to do their thing! By the way, these are progressive influences.

The Greek word *arche* that is translated as the English word "principality" is defined as "a commencement (i.e., *a beginning or doorway*)." It is where the English word "archway" is derived. What are "principalities?" They are demonic spirits that specialize in opening a door of influence in the life of a person in order to gain *entrance* into your life. They are the forces that initiate Satan's processes. They are able beings who know all too well how to stimulate our flesh. They know how to commence an operation of the flesh and open the way for other demonic influences to gain an entrance into our mind. These guys are Satan's Special Forces. These *arche* (*principalities*) open the door for the demonic *exousia* (i.e., *authorities*) to get us to agree with their program. These demonic beings are the spirits that control access once the entrance has been gained. They are the influences that get you to "agree" with what has gained entrance into your life. You see someone who is attractive and they immediately motivate you to have fleshly thoughts about them. Once you have a fleshly thought, the race is on to move you further and further into worldly thinking. They manipulate and deceive us so the *kosmokrator* (*rulers of this world*) can do their work of destruction and manipulation. A *kosmokrator* is a demonic spirit used to establish and promote worldliness and a fleshly approach to a temptation that Satan's method of attack has installed in your mind. *Kosmos* is the Greek word that is defined as the decoration or the adorning of the world. Cosmetology is the art of adorning, or making us look better. New hair-do, new nails, new make-up, new clothes, new cologne, and the like are all staged to attract someone into our influence or for someone to have a better impression of us. These spirits influence a state of mind that diminishes spirituality and promotes fleshliness. I do not see in the Scriptures that it is a sin to put on makeup or to fix your hair; but Satan uses these to gain entrance into our life when he has already got us thinking his way. These demonic spiritual influences also give entrance to wicked spirits in the heavenly realm. These spirits produce "plots of malice," as they are defined and by their definition these spirits are hurtful, degenerative, calamitous, and derelict; as they are defined in the Greek lexicon. This is Satan's method of operation. Satan waits for these forces to fashion and finish an opportunity to create *phobos* (*fear, timidity, or some form of phobia*) in us.

Comprehending Satan's Strategy

Phobos, Pagis, Noema, Pathos, and Oneidismos

The psychological concept of "phobia" comes from the Greek word *phobos*. *Phobeo*, a derivative of *phobos*, is described as the type of fear used to control any person in a given situation. Satan creates a situation and then uses phobias to generate unreasonable or persistent fear or anxiety about common circumstances in order to eliminate an individual's effectiveness or to weaken a person's resolve, which in turn causes them to become vulnerable to additional satanic suggestion. This is where the *pagis* comes in. *Pagis* is translated as the "snare" of the devil in 1 Timothy 3:7, 1 Timothy 6:9, and 2 Timothy 2:26. When Satan sets a *pagis*, which is a trick or a stratagem (i.e., *the temptation*), he is trying to catch us in something. When I was a boy my Dad showed me how to build a rabbit trap. We built a long box, about six inches square, and would put hail wire over one end and a sliding door on the other. We drilled a hole about two-thirds of the way from the door and would put a piece of carrot or celery in the box by the hail wire. We slid a small stick in the hole that had a string tied to the top of it and attached the other end to the door. You could lean the stick back just a bit to hold the door up and we would strategically place it in an area that we had seen rabbits. Then we would walk away and usually buy the next morning we had a rabbit. This is how a pagis works. You put something that is tempting in our minds, like the preverbal carrot, and then wait for us to take the bait. By the time you figure out that it was a trap, it is too late.

> "And *that* they may recover themselves out of the strategy of
> the devil, who are ensnared by the will of *Satan*."
> (2 Timothy 2:26 SNT)

Satan sets these snares through his *noema*. A *noema* is a "device" that is utilized as bait. *Noema* is also translated in the New Testament as "mind" (or *mindset*), also as the word "devices," and "thoughts." *Noema* also means "to perceive." Satan uses his perceptions (i.e., *his knowledge of us*) as bait. He utilizes our fleshly weaknesses to draw us into the temptation and then once we take the bait, he can then bring reproach to us. We will look at how Satan uses reproach a little further in this chapter. If someone has a problem in an area of the flesh, it is Satan's common approach to use it against them. This is why the Bible says "there hath been no temptation taken you but such as is common to man" and the Lord wants you to understand this truth (see 1 Corinthians 10:13). Here are some passages where *noema* is used:

"Unless Satan would get an advantage of us *when we do not forgive others*: because we are not ignorant of his devices (*noema: purposes*; *that is, his mindset and thoughts*)."
(2 Corinthians 2:11 SNT)

"In who the god of this world has blinded their minds (*noema*) who do not believe, unless the light of the glorious gospel of Christ, who is the image of God, would shine in them.."
(2 Corinthians 4:4 SNT)

"But their minds (*noema*) were blinded: because *even* until this *very* day the same veil remains, not being taken away in the reading of the old testament; which *veil* is abolished in Christ."
(2 Corinthians 3:14 SNT)

"Breaking down *conceited* imaginations, and every high thing that exalts itself against the knowledge of God, and bringing into captivity every thought (*noema, purpose, device*) to the obedience of Christ."
(2 Corinthians 10:5 SNT)

In 1 John 4:18, notice that fear (*phobos*) has "torment" attached to it. This "torment" is defined as "self-imposed infliction." This self-imposed punishment will not allow the believer to mature in the faith, and is why Satan uses fear in the first place.

"Because you have not received the spirit of bondage (*slavery*) on the other hand to be afraid (*phobos*); but you have received the Spirit of adoption, through which we cry, Abba (*My Father or Daddy*), Father."
(Romans 8:15 SNT)

Phobos is utilized to create bondage. This bondage is designed to make the believer subject to the controls of Satan. He wants us to act a certain way when he pulls the string.

"And deliver them who through *the* fear (*phobos*) of

death were all *of* their lifetime in the fear of bondage."
(Hebrews 2:15 SNT)

When Satan can achieve fear in us, he can then create *pathos*. *Pathos* comes from the root word that means "a hurt, a wound, or a suffering." *Pathos* is defined as "the soul's diseased condition from which the various lusts spring." Our souls were "damaged" by the fall of man. The undamaged soul does not need to lust. It has great self confidence; not pride. *Pathos* is the "path" someone's mental condition takes because of the state of their inner man. The "*pathos* of a root*" is a problem that produces a longing for sin. If it is not dealt with, one cannot possess his vessel in sanctification and honor (see 1 Thessalonians 4:4). Satan uses his devices to hinder our spiritual growth and development, which come through discipleship. This is why many individuals do not particularly care for discipleship. Satan uses pride to cause us to think we do not need it. We think that reading books or watching videos of different preachers can train our soul, but this is not the case. These things a helpful, but true discipleship occurs when we are held accountable. Accountability is the only way we can wean our soul from the things it wants. You may say, "Are you sure?" Each of us know our own hearts desires. We fight wrong thoughts on a daily basis. If we are accountable, we will have an easier time overcoming our short falls. This is true only when you truly want to change though! Someone convinced against their will, is of a different opinion still. Without personal effort, we will not change. This is why discipleship is so necessary. The problem we face in the modern Church is that very few of them actually disciple. Discipleship is more than Bile study. Bible study is a part of it, but it is the accountability that works miracles. Jesus held the disciples accountable. When their thoughts were wrong, he corrected them. When their faith was small, he corrected them. The soul of mankind hates accountability, but that is why it is so necessary.

Oneidismos is the reproach the devil causes in someone. It is the "self-imposed infliction" that we discussed earlier. It is also the internal taunting, which produces a sense of disgrace. This usually causes the person to have the desire to stop fighting against what they perceive as unfixable and this is Satan's ultimate goal in the warfare; to get us to resign to the temptation. When you refrain from fighting, Satan has one less Saint to worry about.

As believers recognize Satan's schemes and his attempts to weaken them, they should be able to counter his attacks effectively. Recognition is truly one of the major keys to victory. When a believer grows in the admonition of the Lord and develops soldiering skills, they will ultimately mature in the resistance process and be able to hold off and counter demonic attacks. This is the purpose of Christian discipleship and spiritual training.

Comprehending the Spirit of Anti-Christ

"Because many misleaders have entered into the world, who do not acknowledge that Jesus Christ has come in the flesh. This is a misleader and an antichrist."
(2 John 7 SNT)

"Little children, it is the last time: and as you have heard the antichrist will come, even now there are many antichrists; from which we perceive that it is the last time."
(1 John 2:18 SNT)

"Who is a liar except the one that denies that Jesus is the Christ? That person is an antichrist that denies the Father and the Son."
(1 John 2:22 SNT)

"And every spirit that does not acknowledge that Jesus Christ is come in the flesh is not from God: and this is that *spirit* of antichrist, which you have heard that it will come; and presently is already in the world."
(1 John 4:3 SNT)

One of the major areas of concern in Christendom is the Antichrist. Who is he? Where will he come from? What will cause his rise to power? These are all valid questions, but one cannot forget that his spirit has been in the earth and working against the kingdom of God for two thousand years (see 1 John 2:18 and 2 John 1:7). We are closer than ever to the last of the Last Days and the spirit of anti-Christ is very active in today's world and is also in the American society as never before. The book of Revelation foretells his personal manifestation, while the Apostle John makes us aware that the spiritual manifestations of the antichrist have been and are presently operating for almost 2000 years. These anti-Christ manifestations are spiritual in their origin, even though they operate through the soul and flesh of mankind, in and through much of our media, and in many false religions. Demonic forces are spiritual in nature, yet they can usually be recognized as influences on the soul of individuals (i.e., *influences on the mind, will, and temperament of a person*), and can also be seen in anti-Christian rhetoric and anti-Christian attitudes that permeate our society and the world. We should be aware that demonic influences are presently trying to manipulate every area of our society, pushing legislation to outlaw any aspect of God in our culture. Demonic influences continuously try to affect the walk of every believer; even when their influence may be more indirect than direct in many people's lives. As stated in the last section the Greek word *pneuma*, translated as "spirit" in the New Testament can be more clearly defined as that influence which "gives life" to something. The breath of God or the moving of God's Spirit is God's influence on us. God's Spirit gives life to our spirit and the things that are godly, modest, pure, true and virtuous, while the spirit of antichrist produces and gives life to the things that are against Christ and fleshly. The spirit of anti-Christ has been increasing in strength and intensity during the past few decades and his influence is becoming a part of the mainstream of American society. Sin is now so "normal" that when we stand against it, we are the bad guys! When we can differentiate between the influences of demonic manipulation and how their devices affect us, we will then be able to observe how they operate, coerce, and hinder us as individuals. Satan is working to produce a false life in many Christians (i.e., *the life of the flesh*); a temporary thrill. Many people do not recognize the difference between the true life of God and the emotionalism of "consumer" Christianity, which is promoted throughout the Church in our so called modern era. The Scripture states that there is nothing new under the sun and the proponents of the so called "Modern Era" are constantly using this ideology to attack the Church as a whole, as well as individuals. Much of the emotionalism propagated in today's churches is a form of *spiritual* life that is based on temporal things, it only satisfies the impatience of a person's soul, but has no God power that enables Christians to spiritually mature. Oh! The sermons are good, but there is an obvious lack of spiritual power. It consummates in the "I want it now and will do anything to get it" mentality. I have Pastored for over thirty years and am amazed at the number of Christians who fall into the grossest sin, as well as people who struggle with their daily life. It is not just people in the world that are being affected by these demonic schemes, the Church is experiencing open manifestations of false spiritual power that is turning people away from Jesus' original plan and purpose. Paul spoke if this in 2 Timothy 3:5 (SNT).

"Having an appearance of godliness, but contradicting
the power of it: from such turn away."

Three things to notice in this passage: first, the word "appearance" means "a formula, or the semblance of the real." This means that people claim to be Christians, but there is no "form" (*appearance*) of Christ in their lives. They have not changed or they reverted back to their former self, which is what the definition of the word means. They come to church, know the Christian lingo, say the right things, know how to answer the religious and spiritual questions, but the life of Christ is not in them.

Second, the word "contradicting" also means "to deny, to refuse to accept, and/or to reject" the very transforming nature of the gospel. They want to be "saved," but they have left their former relationship with Christ. When a Christian renounces a Christ centered character, and replaces it with attitudes that do not display any of the Holy Spirit's influence; this is how the spirit of anti-Christ reveals himself. When a person's "faith" has no redeeming value, then it is not true Christian faith...it is just religious in nature. It has always been easier for individuals to observe the forms of religion than to bring their heart under the controlling influence of the Holy Spirit. The regular "forms" of religion; church attendance, religious prayers, and doctrinal adherence become a substitute for actual faith in Christ.

The third thing about the passage is that Paul commands us to turn away and avoid such people. This is very of Paul who is looking out for us by warning us about such people. They are a bad influence on those of us who pursue the Lord with all our heart, mind, soul, and strength.

The Scripture says we are "not ignorant of his devices," but what are his devices? A *noema* (*device*) is a perception "i.e., a purpose in one's point of view or, by implication the intellect and disposition one uses to create a perception" in another person. As we have seen before, Satan's devices are his thoughts, and the mindset he creates in us through our perceptions, attitudes, moods, and dispositions. He deceives us into believing that his thoughts and attitudes are our thoughts and attitudes, or that those thoughts and attitudes are the general attitudes and dispositions of the Church and its leaders, thus creating in us an open door of agreement that he can use to gain entrance into our hearts. The only time Satan has power to manipulate us is when we get into agreement with him. Our agreement with God is called confession, while our agreement with the spirit of anti-Christ is called deception (see Luke 21:8). As we reviewed in the previous section, Satan and his demons use a strategy of direct and indirect influences that turn and lead us into their

41

predetermined course. The word *noema* is also used in 2 Corinthians 3:14, when the Scripture states that "their minds (*noema*) were blinded." Satan uses his schemes against our thinking. The Greek word *poroo*, translated as "blinded," gives us a clue as to how Satan worked to accomplish his goal. *Poroo* is defined as "to petrify or harden," but is also where our word "porous" comes from. The Greek root of the word is *poros* and is a kind of stone; a porous stone; one that has the ability to absorb. Part of Satan's strategy is to harden our heart against the spiritual leadings of the Holy Spirit so he can manipulate the truth and bring deception to the "hearer." If I am unable to distinguish between the spiritual influences of Satan and the Holy Spirit, I am weakened and the battle will be lost. Satan attacks us by using the weaknesses and tendencies of our natural being. It is natural for us to want to see miracles and it is natural for us to want to feel spiritual vitality, but the true course of God is to give Jesus the glory and not the miracle or the worker of the miracle. When Satan can utilize familiar or family spirits, it gives him a greater advantage because he utilizes the familiarity of our circumstances to trick and ambush us. This is why custom and tradition are so often Satan's strongest weapons. Think about how Satan used the Pharisees and the Sadducees to work his wickedness against Jesus? The one area they had grown accustomed to, the Law (i.e., *God's Word*), became his tool. He used the same tactic on Jesus when He was led of the Holy Spirit in the wilderness. He tried to get Jesus to agree with him as *he* interpreted the Scripture. Satan did the same thing to Eve. Satan used the custom of the religious tradition to corrupt and pervert the minds of the Sadducees and the Pharisees. Think about this. How did Satan attack the Gentiles as Paul and others came into each town? He did it through the area they were most familiar with; idolatry and self exaltation. The Romans used their personal status to bully and lord over people. They were arrogant. Arrogance is defined as "assuming; making or having the disposition to make exorbitant claims of rank or estimation; giving one's self an undue degree of importance." Satan uses the process of "blindness" as his device to cause people to sift the truth through their tradition, which calluses the heart against the Spirit of God. Isaiah 29:10-14 (KJV) deals this matter from an Old Testament perspective.

"For the Lord has poured out upon you the spirit of deep sleep, and has closed your eyes: the prophets and your rulers, the seers has he covered (*overwhelmed*). And the vision of all is become unto you as

42

the words of a book that is sealed, which men deliver to one that is learned, saying, Read this, I pray thee; and he says, I cannot; for it is sealed: And the book is delivered to him that is not learned, saying, Read this, I pray thee: and he said, I am not learned. Wherefore the Lord said, Forasmuch as this people draw near me with their mouth, and with their lips do they honor me, but have removed their heart far from me, and their fear toward me is taught by the precept of men: Therefore, behold, I will proceed to do a marvelous work among this people, even a marvelous work and a wonder: for the wisdom of their wise men shall perish, and the understanding of their prudent men shall be hid."

The prophet Isaiah is simply saying that when blindness comes upon a people, they cannot understand the Word of God or the moving of His Spirit. They have no personal respect for God and have to be taught reverence, because true faith is not in them. By the way, this is the definition of "ungodliness." It is when people who claim to be Christians have no respect for God in their inner man and have to be taught the things that should have occurred at salvation. They began to pursue things that have no godly meaning and they venture into dead works. When Jesus quoted these verses from Isaiah in Matthew 15:8-11 (SNT), He added this statement,

"But in hollowness *of heart* do they worship me,
teaching *for* doctrines the commandments of men."

Paul also dealt with this in Colossians 2:20-23 (SNT):

"Therefore if you are dead with Christ from the principles of the world, why, as though you are still alive in the world, do you submit to religious dogma, such as (You cannot touch *this or that*; you cannot eat *this or that*; you cannot have anything to do with *this or that*; Which all are perishable in the usage (*idiom: they become dung after they are used*) down to the commandments and doctrines of men? Which some indeed have a show of wisdom in will worship (*the religion of self-will and legalism*), and *through false* humility, and neglecting of the body; in not giving any honor to anyone as though that is satisfying to the flesh."

Isaiah also says,

"For the terrible one is brought to nought, and the scorner is consumed, and all that watch for iniquity are cut off. That make a man an offender for a word, and lay a snare for him that reproveth in the gate, and turn aside the just for a thing of nought."
(Isaiah 29:20-21 KJV)

Isaiah 29:20-21 reveals that "blinded" people make a man an "offender for a word" or they turn aside or do not have relationships with people, because of something that is actually no big deal. They see something that a person does and blow it completely out of proportion because their "religion" prohibits it, and it does not matter to them what the Bible says. I am amazed at how Satan uses religious notions and concepts of holiness to create division and strife in churches and with brothers and sisters in the Lord. The spirit of antichrist substitutes and changes Jesus' purpose into some hyper-spiritual concept of piety that has no eternal value; it causes division and strife under the guise of their religious holiness. The spirit of antichrist uses his influence to manifest a "holier than thou" mentality and manipulates both sides in any issue to support his purpose of division. The real snare occurs when both parties use the Bible to support their individual religious causes.

Satan's skill and experience in the ways of division seems to thwart our individual ability to counter him. Only through the power of discernment, the Holy Spirit, and through the truth of God's Word can we ever experience victory. Though victory is guaranteed to the believer, it is guaranteed only in Jesus Christ. Being a Christian does not automatically mean we have victory in our daily life. We must walk in the Spirit and obedience to Christ if we are to experience it. That is why the Bible says if we walk in the spirit we will not give place to the flesh. Victory is given to those who do God's will and walk in God's ways. All the rest is just religion and Satan uses religion to further his cause. The spirit of error utilizes the selfish nature found in mankind to maintain deception and to promote the causes Satan has designed in his schemes. This is how Satan's strategy works.

Comprehending the Religious Noema

> "Beloved, do not believe every spirit, but examine the
> spirits *to see* if they are from God: because many false
> prophets are gone out into the world...
> We are from God: everyone that knows God listens to us;
> everyone that is not from God does not listen to us. Through
> this we understand *the difference between* the spirit of truth,
> and the spirit of deception."
> (1 John 4:1, 6 SNT)

We must validate the principle of "examining the spirits" in our lives in order for us to walk in victory. The word "examine" simply means "to test, try, or scrutinize" in order to discover the true origin and purpose of the spirit. We are to try every spirit, notion, thought, or idea that comes into our mind to discover its purpose, impact, effect, and origin. Even when Church leaders preach or promote an issue it has to be weighed against the Scriptures. Galatians 2:4 speaks about "false brethren" who bring in hidden agendas, and Jude 4 also says that there are certain men crept in "unawares." Both of these statements indicate that they come into the Body of Christ by stealth. These false ones, the tares, come in alongside the brethren and settle into the Church, no one noticing that they are truly snares to the work of the local church. John said there are many false prophets in the world. John was saying that in his experience he had witnessed many individuals who hindered the work of God's anointing in the Church. John uses the term *antichristos* for some of these people, because he is giving clarity to us that we may better understand the work that the spirit of antichrist performs. The word "antichrist" comes from two Greek root words. The first Greek word in "antichrist" is *anti* and is defined as "to be opposite." It is also defined as meaning both "equivalence" and "exchange." On the positive side of the word, the Scripture states that Christ died *anti* (i.e., *in our stead or in our place*), but when the word is used of the antichrist, it shows how this spirit tries to have equivalence with Jesus by substituting his will over God's Will. The spirit of antichrist disguises itself so that our hearts and minds are deceived into believing in an alternate lord. *Anti* expresses the idea of being "in contrast to," but also means "to be a substitute" for something, or "to be in the place of someone." A demonic spirit is *anti* when it is trying to take Jesus place of lordship by acting as though it is the real Lord. The second word in "antichrist" is *christos* and means "anointed" or "anointing," and comes from the Greek word *chrio*, which is defined "to contact" or "rub, as to smear with oil." By implication, the combined word "antichrist" means "to be opposite or opposed to Christ, due to its desire to be a substitute for, to be in the place of, and to replace the anointing of God with a deceptive and false anointing." In essence, Satan wants to be like the Most High God (see Isaiah 14:14). Satan is a counterfeiter who tries to imitate God by design. This is his *noema* (*his device*). Through this deception he activates his undermining influence and causes many believers to fall short of their potential. We can see how an anti-Christ spirit works in a clearer way by studying the word "divination." The root word in "divination" is divine. When a spirit of divination is at work in a false prophet or a seducer they move over into God's place by speaking as though they are "divine." Instead of speaking for God, they speak as God. The subtlety of this may be difficult for us to catch, but you spirit will let you know that something is wrong. Diviners will give words of prophecy commanding an individual to do something that only God has the authority to dictate. They take God's position of authority over the believer as they speak. They try to rule over and dominate the believer by their words and position. When you look for the life of God on some of these prophesies you do not find it. We had better be careful in the Church and guard whom we let in. And it does not matter how popular they are, how many radio and television stations they are on, or how big their church is. Church leaders should guard their heart so they do not venture into this venue.

When Jesus defeated the devil He empowered us. How? It is through our understanding of what was actually accomplished on the cross. The only counter Satan has for the truth is a lie! Through lies Satan manipulates, deceives, and works to hide his downfall by perverting the truth. The Scripture has revealed that one of Satan's strongest tools is his ability to stealthily act as though he is God. He counters the real work of the Lord with false religious notions. There was a time when we believed that the spirit of antichrist focused on false religions. Islam, Hinduism, Buddhism, and other false religions were and still are used to confuse and manipulate the longing for God that is in every human being. Today the spirit of antichrist is attacking the Church from within as well as from the without. Of course Satan has always attacked the Church and individuals in the pews, but in these Last Days his spirit has developed some effective tactics.

"Because there will arise (*come from obscurity*) false Christs (*pretend Messiahs or saviors*), and false (*pretend*) prophets, and will show (*minister*) great signs (*miracles or indications of their reality*) and wonders (*different aspects of miracles*); insomuch that, if *it were* possible, they will *even* deceive (*seduce*) the very elect (*remnant*). Behold, I have told you before."
(Matthew 24:24-25 SNT)

"Be discreet, be a diligent watcher; because your adversary the devil, just as a roaring lion *seeking his prey*, walks about, plotting who he can devour: Whom *you must* resist steadfastly in the faith, knowing that the same hardships are endured by your brothers that are in the *rest of the* world."
(1 Peter 5:8-9 SNT)

The Greek word translated as "adversary" (*antidikos*) comes from two root derivatives. We have already looked at the word *anti*, but the second word *dike* means to "be right (*as self-evident; i.e., justice; the principle, a decision, or its execution*)." The word "adversary," therefore indicates in the original language "that someone is against our rightness and justification" or is someone or something that tries to "substitute," or "take the place of" our true position in Christ." We must realize that God named our enemy. The Lord called him Lucifer, which means "to make a show, to boast, or to be prideful." When Lucifer manifests in the life of an individual, you will recognize it as pride, as a boastful disposition, and leads to someone who makes an open show of their person for the purpose of exalting themselves over you. This manifests through "the pride of life" that Jesus spoke of. The Lord named him Satan, because this means "the accuser of the brethren" or "the opponent of the brethren." Satan manifests himself through a person's life by using an accusative and contrary attitude. We can see this manifestation in people who criticize and degrade the Church, or individuals in it. Our enemy is also called the devil, because he is a deceiver. He is a manipulator and a worker of evil. He works in stealth to cover his tracks and to place the blame on anything or anyone else. This is our enemy. If we let our guard down he uses his deception as a device to weaken and then destroy us. When Paul used the word "device" in 2 Corinthians 2:11 it was in the context that Satan uses unforgiveness to get an advantage over us. This is not to say that we are to overlook sin, but it is to say that we are to love one another enough to help each other when we see that someone is weak or under attack and to have grace

47

for the unstable soul. We should forgive every offence, no matter how deeply it hurt us. We know God will bring every wrong to light at the Judgment. We may not forget the offence, but we surely should forgive it.

> "But if our gospel is hid, it is hidden to the ones that are
> lost: In who the god of this world has blinded their
> minds who do not believe, unless the light of the
> glorious gospel of Christ, who is the image
> of God, would shine in them."
> (2 Corinthians 4:3-4 SNT)

I have been researching the biblical concept of "lost-ness" and I have only heard the word "lost" (*in the Christian vernacular*) used in the context of those who do not know Jesus as their Lord and Savior. In my research of the Bible I have discovered that "lost-ness" has an Old Testament root. The Greek word *apollumi* (*lost*) literally means to "destroy" or "kill" in battle. Figuratively it is used in relation to the soul. The soul is an object of value to the Lord in which He is interested in saving. The Jewish expression for "lost-ness" was that a man could "trifle away his life" by bad personal choices. The Jewish thought was that one was "lost" when they suffered a loss that was attributable to their foolish will or was the fault of the one who suffered it. This does not mean that he destroys himself with suicide, but that he did not keep himself pure from the influences of the world that lead him into loss. In Luke 15, three parables are told from God's point of view: the lost sheep, the lost coin, and the lost son. It is God who sees their lost-ness in these passages. The sheep's lost-ness occurs when they leave their pasture and shepherd, not because they have no pasture or shepherd. The coin's lost-ness occurred when it was separated from the whole and was not useful to its master. The son's lost-ness occurred when he took his inheritance and used it to enter into riotous living; he squandered his inheritance, in other words. We, as sheep, become lost when we leave God and His ways. We are lost, as the coin, when we are no longer useful to our Master. And like the son, we are lost when we take our inheritance of eternal life and squander it on worldliness.

Psalm 119:176 gives us a pure definition of lost-ness as well as Isaiah 53:6, and Jeremiah 50:6.

> "I have gone astray like a lost sheep; seek thy servant;

for I do not forget thy commandments."
(Psalm 119:176 KJV)

"All we like sheep have gone astray; we have turned everyone to his own way; and the Lord has laid on him the iniquity of us all."
(Isaiah 53:6 KJV)

"My people hath been lost sheep: their shepherds have caused them to go astray, they have turned them away on the mountains: they have gone from mountain to hill, they have forgotten their resting place."
(Jeremiah 50:6 KJV)

In Ezekiel 34:4, God is critical of the shepherds who do not search for those who are "lost," while verse sixteen contrasts this criticism with the statement, "I will seek that which is lost." The Bible then states in Ezekiel 34:17, "I will judge between cattle and cattle, between rams and he goats." And again in Ezekiel 34:20-22 and 31 (KJV) it is stated:

"Therefore thus saith the Lord God unto them; Behold, I, even I, will judge between the fat cattle and between the lean cattle. Because you have thrust with the side and with the shoulder, and pushed all the diseased with your horns, till you have scattered them abroad. Therefore will I save my flock, and they shall no more be prey; and I will judge between cattle and cattle...
And you my flock, the flock of my pasture, are men and I am your God, saith the Lord God."

In essence, the Bible is revealing that lost-ness is not merely a term that relates to those outside the people of God (*as traditional doctrines teach*), it also applies to those who know God, but have moved away from Him in their hearts. Lost-ness is also seen in the context of those that have been "run off from church." The Bible reveals that there are those in the Body of Christ who are immature and have ruinous ways (i.e., *they are lost*). They are lost from the reality of Christian love and true communion, because they are lost from Christian fellowship and friendship. They are lost in a crowd of believers and feel alone and abandoned. They are lost from maturity, because maturity only comes through building wholesome Christian relationships. False shepherds and tares will bully God's people when the spirit of antichrist deceives them. They are like a mean ram

49

in the field; they butt everything that gets in their way. Ministers may view their ways as promoting holiness, but their actions are not Christ-like; as Ezekiel states. These "shoulder thrusters" may think that they are preaching against sin and confronting sin, but in reality Satan has used a *noema* in them to embitter God's people by their preaching and haughtiness.

"Because you have had a perpetual hatred, and have shed the blood of the children of Israel by the force of the sword in the time of their calamity, in the time that their iniquity had an end."
(Ezekiel 35:5 KJV)

Ezekiel is warning us to be discerning. If someone is young in the Lord and fails, they should be handled respectfully, even during correction. Immaturity means their iniquity has "an end" as Ezekiel states. In Texas terms if they are flexible, adaptable, and correctable then they are capable of change. When a young brother or a sister is struggling in some area of their life, we should not use the "force of the sword" (*the Word of God*) in the time of their calamity; we are to walk them through the recovery process. The "force of the sword" does not recover, heal, and change the person; the sword under these circumstances wounds and destroys. It is the goodness of God that leads us to repentance and it is the goodness of God that will help the weak to overcome. Satan has used these religious devices to hinder the maturity and unity of the Church long enough.

"And then *at that time* will many be offended (*tripped up and snared*), and will betray one another, and will be hateful *toward* one another. And many false (*pretend*) prophets will rise (*come from obscurity*), and will deceive (*mislead*) many. And because iniquity (*wickedness*) will abound (*increase*), the love of
many will become spiritually insensitive."
(Matthew 24:10-12 SNT)

Notice that the false prophets shall "rise." The Greek word "rise" is defined as "to collect one's faculties, to awaken from obscurity or inactivity." These false ones come out of a time when offense, hatred, and betrayal are in the religious world. The Greek word *skandalizo*, translated as "offended" and is defined as "to trip up, to entrap, or to entice to sin." It is where the English word "scandalize" comes from and this word is a derivative of the Greek word *skandalon* which is the "trap-stick" in a snare we discussed earlier.

Some doctrines snare you. *Skandalon* in the Greek language is a bent sapling that is used as a trigger to set a snare. Just like the trap stick I used in my rabbit cage. Satan uses snares to catch us in a strategic scheme. He wants to divide us. We are weak when we are in division so his goal is to keep us divided. He has been using racism, denominationalism, and ignorance to separate us from one another throughout history. The Bible also states that the love of the Church will "become spiritually insensitive." To "become spiritually insensitive" is to maintain an attitude of giving up on the people of God. The spirit of antichrist utilizes and promotes this coldness of Christian love to produce strands of separation within the local church and in the universal Church as well. Correction is necessary in the Body of Christ and a mild rebuke can go a long way in correcting these attitudes, but again, it must be done respectfully. Wisdom brings a balance between the correction that is necessary and the seriousness of a rebuke. Wisdom in these matters is the principle thing.

Christians in today's Church have been duped on occasion by false theology and doctrine so that their understanding of the antichrist has been limited. Some doctrines have the anti-Christ manifesting only in the tribulation, which perverts the reality of his presence today. The spirit of antichrist is very active and present in our world. It is operating inside and outside of the Church and he is using the political systems in the Church and in the country for his own benefit. The spirit of antichrist is continuously working to undermine Christ Jesus and the kingdom of God by distorting the truth. He will manifest openly someday, but in this present time we should be aware of his influence. It is time for the Church to see him and his ministry for what it is. It is time to prepare yourself for the spiritual battle that is at hand.

Printed in Great Britain
by Amazon.co.uk, Ltd.,
Marston Gate.